UNIVERSAL LANGUAGE BASE

Also by Vera Dragilyova

IDEASTHESIA

SPEAKING STARTER KIT

THE UNKNOWN UNKNOWNS

INTUITIVE MEDICINE

UNIVERSAL LANGUAGE BASE

Learn a Foreign Language Like a Child

Vera Dragilyova

Verarta Books

CONTENTS

INTRODUCTION

Our first language is not something we deliberately learn. It is something that happens to us, when we are a child. Learning a language as an adult is different: we start by looking at rules and grammar, with minimal exposure to the spoken language and culture,—which too often results in failure.

However, your learning story can have a happy end. If we feed language to our brain the way it likes it, it will learn it with pleasure. Otherwise, language is treated as a foreign invader and will be fought and rejected with all might.

In a format of a lean guide, the book focuses on the preparation for language learning, which makes subsequent grammar learning infinitely easier. The preparation is a simulation of every child's initial exposure to language. By the time the reader goes through all the stages of preparing the brain for the traditional study, the brain will be ready to devour all the information provided to it.

This is about giving the brain what it already wants, by first convincing it that it wants it. It is just like marketing: it is easier to sell something that someone already needs than trying to convince them that they need it.

The book proposes a notion of Relevance Principle—certain conditions that will make the brain want to learn a new language, also discussing what hormones motivate language learning. Then, the book covers a sequence of learning stages that starts with passive learning and progresses to the point of delving into grammar.

Further, the book briefly discusses the author's theory of Universal Language base that powers all grammars in the world, and why it is important as a reference for language learners. The theory describes an underlying cognitive model that all humans seem to have, while our brains naturally search for its reflection in the stream of sounds that surround us, allowing it to create a system that we call language.

Finally, the book provides powerful yet simple active learning techniques, including a basic starter kit of grammar that one can use to ease into any language, avoiding being overwhelmed. A few words on translation and interpretation finish the book.

If you can speak one language—you can speak them all!

MY STORY

Growing up in Western Ukraine, when it was still a part of the Soviet Union, we all learned Ukrainian and Russian, as well as local Ukrainian dialects and some Polish. It is in the Carpathian Mountains of Western Ukraine that you will find the geographical center of all Europe, a place that has survived the Ottoman rule, the Austro-Hungarian empire, and the Soviet regime. Each period of its history brought with it immigrants: Armenians, Tatars, Jews, Germans, Greeks, Bulgarians, Hungarians, Gypsies, Romanians, Tatars, Swedes, the French, the Polish, the Dutch, and even Scotts—

just to name a few. Ukraine has always been a place of cultural and linguistic mixture.

Speaking Russian, Ukrainian and Polish, as a child, I simply thought that they were just different ways of saying the same thing. I did not grow up separating one language from another, but not mixing them, either. They were more like word synonyms. For me, just like for others, each language had its own purposes: it was spoken in certain contexts and with certain people, or in a certain mood. Inserting a few words from another language (code-switching) was done for emphasis or for humor, but not because poor knowledge.

My mother was an English teacher, and sometimes professor, so I heard English all the time, but no one ever taught it to me at home. It just rubbed off on me, somehow. In fact, this rubbing off is the most important step in language learning, discussed later in the book. What rubbed off on me, I taught to my mother's students, when she was not available, acting as a substitute teacher since the age of 10. How was that possible? Because I was constantly exposed to spoken English, my brain already had assimilated it. Then, all I had to do was look at the grammar rules that my mom prepared for the students, and they instantly made sense to me. Having understood them myself, I would then teach them to the students. That simple.

When I was little, I tried to study Spanish grammar, but it was unbearably tedious. Going straight to grammar felt like force-feeding and violating my brain, despite my numerous attempts. Teaching someone grammar rules was completely different: it was more like a game, and therefore painless. Doing it alone just didn't feel right. So, teaching my mom's students actually was fun, but teaching myself—my brain would instantly go into a daydreaming zone.

Nothing has changed since my childhood: I am still a lazy grammar learner—the only type of laziness I allow myself! Yet, it is this linguistic laziness that turned out to be my best tool in language learning! How so? By not being afraid, by never trying too hard, I allowed my brain to do what it does naturally and gracefully—absorb a language without my conscious interference. I studied several languages in college, sometimes 3 at the same time, and just opened myself up to them, embraced the culture that gave them birth, and enjoyed all the lessons as something wondrous, without worrying and being afraid of the unknown. Relaxation, curiosity, and playfulness were what helped me.

Because of my personal multi-lingual experience, as well as many observations of bilingual and trilingual children at school, I would encourage parents to teach their children several languages at the same time. Most children, most likely, will not get confused, since for the child's brain, languages are parallel universes that do not intersect, unless deliberately forced to.

Moreover, I am a different person in each language I speak, and how I feel about the other person in a particular context will instantly direct me to what language to choose for communication. I have friends who communicate with me in 5 different languages, and it is great fun! When I am stressed, I can only speak English or Arabic. It is because English is a concrete, concise, direct and thrifty language, when it comes to words and syllables, and a low sound to meaning ratio. Compared to other languages, English feels stripped of emotion, which helps it to be neutral and matter-of-fact.

When I am relaxed, I like to speak Russian. Russian is long-winded, complex, loaded, inflexible, clunky, but is unparalleled in its ability to express emotion, in the most nuanced ways. Especially, when it comes to affection. Only in Russian can you have ten or twenty different endearment versions of one's first name. And they are all grammatically right! You can instantly tell what the speaker is feeling toward you, just from the suffix they choose for your name. That is impossible in nearly all languages of the world, except Romance languages like Spanish and Italian. Iranian, Chinese and some other Asian languages add a "jan" or "chan" at the end of a name, but that is incomparable to the whole universe of endearment built into the Russian grammar.

One question that everyone always asks me is where I am from—just after hearing my accent. They can't place it, and neither can I—to be honest. The matter is that it is artificial: I created my accent when I was little, for aesthetic purposes. It takes about a year to lose one's accent as a child, after immigrating to a new country. During my first year in the United States, I was in High School, and my class-mates encouraged me not to lose my accent. It might have been because I was the only curiosity in town at that time, being the only-non American that first year. Well, as far as I can remember it. They told me that they liked how soft it sounded, so I tried my best to keep it. So, until this day, after having lived in the United States most of my life, I still get questions about where I am from, and it is obvious that people assume that I am "fresh off the boat"! It's nice.

My first course in English in an American High School was in Modesto, CA, in the same High

School where George Lucas studied, and I was always proud to know that. I was put into an Advanced English Literature class, out of my own desire. On the first day, I could not understand a word! The teacher had a heavy Texan accent, and I seriously doubted this was the right room and time, because this could absolutely not have been English! With time, listening and listening to her speak, I suddenly started understanding her, and ended up getting an A in the class. Just relaxing into the situation, instead of stressing, was the key to overcoming this linguistic barrier, I think. My brain did all the work, without my knowing it.

Another reason some people keep their accent is their attachment to their original cultural identity. The less they want to give it up, the more their accent will persist. Accent is usually a great indicator of one's mentality. Some people completely give up their old identity and forget their native language within a mere year. Some people keep both, but they are a minority, in my experience. It seems that the brain does not like having more than one linguistic and cultural identity, unless one grows up that way. It tends to make a choice in favor of one or the other, and then stick to it. Although, there are people who are good at imitating sounds, and their accent has little to do with their identity, but more with their affinity to imitating sounds. In my case,— I have an accent in every single language I speak. Moreover, it changes greatly, depending on my mood,—just like my handwriting does!

One particular experience of learning a foreign language is worth sharing. This is where my linguistic laziness served me well, by not interfering with the way of learning that is more natural for the brain, and therefore, much more effective than simply memorizing lists of words and rules. Some years ago, I studied Egyptian culture and traveled to Egypt several times. During that time, both in the US and in Egypt, I was constantly exposed to the spoken Egyptian dialect of Arabic. Studying literary Arabic called "fos'ha", that is being taught in all schools and universities, is nearly useless for travel and communicating with the locals, since nobody speaks it. People write in it—yes. However, in each Arabic country, people speak their local dialect, which is sometimes so different from other dialects that they are mutually unintelligible, qualifying them to be separate languages, by definition. For example, Egyptians could never understand Moroccans, simply because the vocabulary is too different. Moroccans, on the other hand, could understand Egyptians, only because of the Egyptian film industry that has dominated the Arab world since the second half of the twentieth century.

So, the Egyptian dialect of Arabic was not taught anywhere when I studied Arabic "fos'ha", and no one, absolutely no one wanted to teach it to me. The speakers were either saying that it was impossible to learn. Or maybe, they just did not want me to be privy to their world through understanding their language? Or simply did not have the patience? Or maybe—they could not explain things, since there is a big difference between being able to speak a language and being able to teach it. In any case, I was on my own. I listened and listened to the people's conversations, burning with desire to understand what all the fuss was about. Egyptians tend to be very emotional and expressive, which aids greatly in learning their language, by firing up one's curiosity as to the drama that is taking place. I could read their body language, and started noticing that certain words went along with certain gestures, although, I did not know what they meant precisely.

One fine morning in Egypt, I woke up and opened my mouth to say something. To my great surprise, it all came out in Egyptian Arabic! This is not a joke, nor is this a fake story. This really happened to me, and I remember the feeling like as if I were there right now. I could not believe my ears or the sensation that my mouth was sending to me. How? From where? That moment was a moment of epiphany, an empirical proof of what the human brain is capable of. I understood that day, to an infinite degree of certainty, that language is not something we learn, but it is something that happens to us.

Since then, I have not learned any new languages to the extent that I did Arabic. Arabic got really stuck to me, to the point where it temporarily replaced all fluency in all of my other languages. As a teenager, I had already learned my 6 languages to the level of fluency: Russian, Ukrainian, English, Spanish, French, and Italian. When Arabic happened to me, it is was as if it just undid all of them. It took me about a year to get back to normal. Later I went on to study about 60 languages, but never reached fluency in any of them to the degree that I would like. There are 20 languages that I find most useful, just by virtue of how many speakers they have and how prominent their cultures are. They are also most spoken in the countries where travel is most developed.

These are the 20 languages of my choice:

1 Russian
2 English
3 Spanish
4 French
5 Italian
6 German
7 Egyptian Arabic
8 Portuguese
9 Mandarin Chinese
10 Norwegian
11 Hebrew
12 Turkish
13 Greek
14 Japanese
15 Thai
16 Malay
17 Hindi
18 Farsi
19 Swahili
20 Tagalog

This is not a rating of importance but of practicality. In addition, there is a number of languages that open door to whole linguistic families, like Norwegian, Russian, and Spanish. Learning Norwegian will allow the speaker to get by in both Sweden and Denmark. Russian will open doors to most of the Eastern Europe and even Mongolia. Spanish, which is already spoken all over the planet, will also get you going in Portugal and Brazil.

Anyone can learn the basics of all those languages, enough to get by. And that—is the first step in becoming fluent polyglot.

THE EASIEST LANGUAGE

As long as you learn them all together as a child, all languages are equally easy to learn. However, once you learn your first native language, learning another one later in life is a completely different story, affected by various factors.

One such factor is the nature of your native language, which will bias you tremendously toward liking languages that are similar to yours in structure and vocabulary. Interestingly, there are strange exceptions. If the foreign language you are learning is too similar to your first language, it will be difficult to learn. Since you already are able to understand a lot of it, your brain will not consider it important enough to burden itself with learning it. The main guideline for the brain is "good enough", and if you can understand and communicate well enough to get along in any new language, that is just "good enough" for your brain, and no further action will be taken.

This can happen with learning any n'th language. For me, as a Russian native speaker, learning Portuguese has been extremely difficult. I understand it so well that I don't feel that feverish internal drive to learn it. I can also speak Spanish, and the speakers of Portuguese understand me. Bingo! There is no impetus to drive the language acquisition.

Another situation is when a foreign language is extremely different from your native one. For example, Chinese for native English speakers. You could feel fearful or fascinated with the unknown, but your brain will protest against a very dissimilar language, and will treat it as an invader and aggressor to be battled against. Languages somewhere in the middle will have a better chance of being accepted for learning. It is even more interesting to point out that human attraction works on an analogous principle, where pheromones that signal to us people with extremely similar genetic background (like siblings, parents, and children) feel repulsive, just as those that carry extremely different genetic material from ours. It is exactly the same with languages!

Another factor is attraction to the sounds, or the culture, or even the idea of the language. Many people like the sound of French, which serves a natural motivation for them to learn it. Often not enough, but it is a head start. Many people learn a language because they already like the culture, and would like to assimilate and immerse themselves in it, which is virtually impossible without learning the language. Others might like a language because of the role it has played in history: maybe it is the language of their favorite philosopher or author, and they prefer to read the books in the original. It is good to review such reasons, even if to refresh one's own motivation. Motivation always helps!

Finally, the share the complexity of grammar is also a factor. Any native English speaker who ever studied Latin, will have a reaction at a mere memory of having to memorize all the seemingly useless endings that just don't exist in English grammar. Interestingly, Chinese is one of the most feared languages in the West, yet, it has one of the simplest grammars in the world. What is scary about it? It is the written characters and the tones, both of which serve as a barrier for foreigners. In addition, a lot is understood from the context, so the speakers need to learn the culture, without which the meaning is often impossible to access. Russian has many conjugations and declensions, in addition to ever-mutating word sequence in a sentence which changes meaning. In addition, there are suffixes and other separate particles which have no direct translation into most languages of the world. Learning when and how to use them, and what emotion they carry is an art in itself. Spanish, I find, is the optimal candidate for the first foreign language to learn, with the simplest grammar, which alleviates memorization, no tones, a straightforward orthography, and an uncomplicated Latinate alphabet. It is even easier than English, which has too many exceptions, in all of its aspects of grammar.

The best news is that, once your brain learns how to learn a foreign language, it will transfer its skills to an unlimited number of new languages. The first time is always the hardest. It is all uphill from here—in a good sense.

TRICKING THE BRAIN

Why do some people struggle to learn a few words in a foreign language, and others quickly and easily pick up anything? There are three major reasons in adults: lack of emotional openness, overthinking things, and going straight into learning grammar without any mental preparation. The good news is that there are loopholes to trick the brain into opening up to learning a foreign language.

Emotional Openness.

Education, in general, feels like a violent act to the brain. People are resistant to change, and a new language is one of the top things that the brain despises inviting to enter inside. Our poor ability to learn a foreign language is only a testament of how protective our brain is of our wellbeing. It is our guard against being open to mental assaults, and therefore against going mad.

Children are extremely open and even in need of learning a language, and once it is done, the slot is filled and the need is no longer there. With age, you don't lose an ability to learn. You simply strengthen your ability to protect yourself from a foreign language invasion. If human adults were extremely open to new languages, they would also be extremely vulnerable emotionally, which evolution has sifted out of the human genome long time ago. So, if it is hard for you to learn a foreign language, don't worry—it is all for your won protection, and in the game of the survival of the fittest—you are one of the fittest.

However, humans differ in their degree of protection. Your foreign language learning ability has less to do with your linguistic ability and more with your personality. Your ability to speak your native language is your ability to speak any of the existing language. It is not about that: it is more about opening up to a new world, a new mentality, once you have established your first one as a child.

Openness, sensitivity, empathy and adventurousness are crucial in language acquisition. People who need to stay in control have a harder time opening up to a foreign language. Language takes over and reformats the brain, and once it enters, it is impossible to undo, and it is difficult to predict what effect it will have. Of course, we are wired to be afraid of a new language: it is the fear of the unknown! For an adult, it is assuming a new identity, creating a new self, beyond the point of no return.

To think of it, language learning is all about empathy, which is not being afraid of another human being, of the way they think and feel, even if it is very different from ours. It is about shedding all pre-judgment, and it is this kind of an open mind that it takes to ease your way into a language you want to learn. A language is learned through mirroring others: not just the sounds, but the body language and the accompanying emotion. Empathy is the only tool that can tell you anything about anyone else. There is no other way on earth! The more we can feel what the other person feels, the better we can learn their language.

Not Overthinking.

Trying too hard to learn a language is like trying too hard to relax: it is counterproductive. Thinking is what gets on the way of learning a foreign language. Thinking of what do say next, of whether you are right or wrong, of what others might think of you. Any thinking in language learning is overthinking. Deliberate, conscious, controlled thinking that is. That kind of thinking is only the tip of the iceberg, compared to how much work your brain actually does in the background. By deliberately analyzing everything, especially in the very beginning of learning a language, gets on the way of learning, on the way of your brain's doing its job. Just try to stop thinking and see what your brain and body will do: they will do all the learning on their own, without telling you.

Copying is an essential part of learning a language. Not only empathy helps this process, but also relaxing and avoiding deliberate thought. When you hear some completely new and difficult expression in a foreign language, try to copy it. It is hard, right? You might sound foolish and be afraid to do it ever again. Now, try to copy it without thinking, just copy it like a parrot, for the fun of it! What happens? Suddenly, you can do it and do it perfectly! Why? Because you relaxed and allowed your brain do what it is wired to do, without getting on its way.

Why are children so good at learning computers? Computers are just another language, an interface, and children are not afraid of making mistakes. They don't think—they just try things and see what happens. That is exactly what adults must do in order to learn a language. They have to suspend the fear of being wrong and the conscious effort to be right. Because in language learning there is no right and wrong—there is just do or not do.

Learning with the body.

Learning a language is the same as learning to ride a bicycle or play piano: your whole body is involved, and you couldn't possibly micromanage every movement.

The way that a child learns its native spoken language is kinesthetic—through experiencing the world with the body, and no books, writing, reading are necessary. It happens through reading the nonverbal behavior of others, through observing physical actions taking place, and through the feelings that arise in the child as a result.

So, if a mother makes a happy face, which registers as pleasure in the child, and says a certain word, the child will automatically learn that it is something good. If the father points to the dog and says "doggie", the child will automatically learn the word dog. If the child sees its parents arguing, and they call each other names, the child will automatically learn those words, and know that they mean something bad. It is all about pairing physical and emotional events with a sequence of sounds.

What a child can do, the adult can do, too. We are just brainwashed to think that the way to learn a foreign language is through memorization of rules and vocabulary. No, that comes much later,—after the adult brain has accepted the language into its realm and made it its own. First, the brain needs to hear and observe how a language is used in real life, all the way to internalizing it into the body. Only then the brain is ready to learn the grammar.

RELEVANCE PRINCIPLE

From the very beginning, you need to convince the brain that this new language you are learning is important and worthy of its attention. A language must remain maximally relevant for the brain, before, during, and even after your deliberate study it.

If the brain is convinced, it will continue doing most of the learning on its own, even without your knowing it. If it is not convinced, there is nothing you can do to make it retain any of it. Absolutely nothing! Which is exactly what happens with most of us at school, because before learning a new language, we don't take this crucial necessary step of convincing.

So, how do we convince the brain to learn a new language? I call this the Relevance Principle, where what seems important to the brain will automatically gets its attention. There are many reasons why the brain will consider something important. They are: passive and active repeated exposure, curiosity, and human hormones involved in survival, games, and human relations. Making a language relevant to the brain is important before and during study, as well as thereafter, in order to retain what you have learned.

Passive repeated exposure.

This is the minimum you need, in order to study any language. If you want to keep your brain interested in a language, it must be continually exposed to it, and you don't even have to be actively listening. The exposure can be merely having it on the background for long periods of time, whether you stage it yourself, or are immersed in the environment, where the language is spoken.

Passive repeated exposure is when a foreign language comes to you: you hear it or you see it written, while you do not invest any effort into understanding it. At first, your brain will reject it as something unimportant. Then, it will reject it as something potentially harmful. Then, it will register something it does not understand enough times to consider it relevant and important to grasp,—again, because it is potentially harmful. In order to protect itself, it will try to figure it out.

So, for example, if you find yourself in a foreign country, constantly hearing foreign speech, your brain will automatically tune in and start dissecting the barrage of sounds that is coming its way—and you will not even know. While you are thinking of other things, maybe even speaking to yourself in your native language, you subconscious brain is working hard to detect patterns, make sense, systemize and decipher all of the sounds it is registering. Moreover, it is correlating these sounds with people's gestures and facial expressions, with the time of day and the weather, and with everything it knows about you and what you did today. It is essentially data-mining! A really difficult job. One day, it will figure it out and let you know. Then, suddenly, you might even start understanding what people are saying, but before then—just relax and go on with your business as usual.

Active repeated exposure.

This is where you are repeatedly interacting with a foreign language speaker—regardless of whether you actually speak that language. The main factor is your effort to communicate, using the foreign language. Your mere frustration with the inability to say anything pushes your brain to learn. Your searching the right word, your trying to figure out what the other speaker says, trying to read their facial expression and gestures—all of it promotes foreign language learning.

What differentiates active repeated exposure is having a goal of communication, which masters and streamlines the brain's energy to learn.

Curiosity Hook.

One very powerful factor to incite learning a foreign language is the brain's natural curiosity. Human brain's weakness is in curiosity. It is like a drug to the brain! By asking a question, you cajole the brain to look for an answer. It is a little like when you say not to think of a white elephant: one has to think about it in order not to think about it.

Human brain is a curiosity machine. When you are surrounded by people, having conversations in a language you don't understand, you instinctually yearn to figure out what they are saying. Your brain is jolted with a desire to learn the unfamiliar language as soon as possible. Such a situation appeals not only to your curiosity, but also to your emotions: feeling included, feeling equal to others, and an instinct to socialize.

An analogous situation happens during watching films in a foreign language. Since the brain poorly detects the difference between physical reality and the reality on the screen, a movie simulates the same conversation that you would normally experience in real life.

Additionally, any type of a mystery or a question that requires your knowledge of a foreign language serves as a strong impetus for your brain to learn that language. For example, if you like playing detective in life, and there is a word that would complete the puzzle—that would naturally elevate the status of the word to urgent, and will make your brain search for a translation and then retain it very well. If someone you like writes something in a foreign language, you will be dying to know what it means. If you are trying to solve an ancient archeological puzzle, if you get abducted by aliens and see something written on their foreheads—hypothetically, all of it would make your brain learn much faster. Everything is possible!

Survival and Adrenaline

Having to speak a language in order to survive is the most powerful tool for language learning. It jolts your brain into learning quickly whatever needs to be understood and spoken, in order to survive. Adrenaline is the hormone that prods your brain to do it. If you can simulate or actually put yourself in a situation, where something is at stake and depends on your knowledge of a foreign language,—you are sure to get quick results. Games are an example where both stress and pleasure are in play, to stimulate your brain to start learning. However, going to a country where no one speaks your native language is the easiest way to create a situation of survival. When you have to say the right word to eat, your brain will summon all its power to make you learn what it is and say it well enough to be understood.

Games and Endorphins

Language learning actually makes you happy! Yes!

Language learning stimulates the production of endorphins, flooding nucleus accumbens with pleasure, every time you win in a game, but also every time you succeed in understanding or have someone else understand you in a foreign language. Communicating in a foreign language itself is a game: an unpredictable challenge of someone's saying something to you, and then your searching for the right thing to say in response. Just like playing tennis! Or any other sport. When you engage yourself in any other game that is played in a foreign language, you add yet another layer of motivation. There is an element of survival in every game, where winning is surviving.

The pleasure that endorphins cause you to experience during games, as well as during successful communication in a foreign language, acts as an incredible motivation for the brain to learn.

Love, Friendship, and Oxytocin

Oxytocin is one of the dominant hormones during infancy that ensures child's development, including their language acquisition. Learning in a safe and loving environment eliminates the fight-or-flight response that blocks any kind of learning. A relaxing environment also lets a person take their guards down, so that their emotional filter is not blocking the incoming unknown information.

When you are able to connect and communicate with a friend or a lover, or a friendly stranger, you get a rush of oxytocin, which makes you feel warm and fuzzy inside. Pleasure is a major indicator to the brain that something is relevant and important. Pleasure rewards your brain for its effort to learn a language, and motivates it to keep learning.

Moreover, your attitude toward a language can be acquired through your experience with its originating culture, or personal experiences with the speakers of this language. If you had a memorable positive episode with speakers of Amharic, for example, you might start being attracted to Ethiopian culture, and enjoying the language, always having flashbacks to those great moments, and creating images in your head of how Ethiopia is. Then, your brain will become biased in favor of learning Amharic, if you ever decide to in the future.

On the other hand, if someone with a strong accent from a particular country is rude to you even once, you might acquire and unpleasant taste for the native language of that speaker, or even dislike the whole country, just based on this one incidence. It will make you biased against learning that language in the future. I remember, in college, I disliked my professor of German, only because she had a habit of dismissing my questions as irrelevant. In retrospect, I think that she just did not know the answers, but her condescending tone made me feel so frustrated and disrespected that I formed a blockage against German. Until now, I feel uneasy about learning German, although I really like Germany. Turning your brain biased for or against a certain language, based on life experiences, the sound of the language, or the degree of its similarity to your native one,— can either torpedo or thwart your entire effort of learning that language in the future.

5 STAGES OF PASSIVE EXPOSURE

Ideally, you would be passively and actively exposed to that language, by hearing it on the background and by interacting with a native speaker, before you embark on your study of a foreign language the traditional way. Ideally, you would be talking and playing games in a foreign language with the person you love, or surviving in a jungle, with only the natives around you, who would demand a word in their native language from you, in exchange for food. However, if you are unable to find any native speakers for interaction, passive exposure alone is a powerful preparation tool.

Every child is attuned to the patterns in the incoming stimuli from all five human senses. Initially, a child who can hear, is exposed to language through listening, and language learning happens without any special effort. This is what passive exposure is. As adults, we can simulate such exposure, to take advantage of the inborn linguistic powers of our brain.

Passive exposure is quintessential to language study, and the minimum you need to get started. Games, curiosity, survival, and relationships can all greatly augment your learning potential, but passive learning is simply irreplaceable.

Language is not something you study, but it is something that happens to you. Then, after it happens to you, you can study it, to make sense of what you have learned, and acquire more. But before then, you have to relax and let the brain do its job. Skipping the pre-study step is signing your impossibility certificate.

So, what is this crucial preliminary step? It consists of several stages of exposure, during which the brain will start learning the language on its own, without any conscious effort on your part. Remember what happened to me with Arabic? I woke up one day and started speaking! This may not happen to everyone, and this crucial preparation is not a replacement for language learning. It is only a period when the brain does its language learning before you start your own, the traditional way. If you skip this step, you will most likely waste a lot of time in painful memorization, or you might even give up, if your brain turns out to be very protective of you and does not allow a foreign language invader in, without proper treatment. Not that no one ever learned any language strictly the traditional way: of course, they have. However, if you have difficulty learning the traditional way, it is very likely that your stubbornly protective brain is the culprit. So, just give some special treatment, do it the nice way, and you will thank yourself later.

This special treatment is what I call Learning from Scratch, and it consists of five stages of exposure, where the brain accumulates its knowledge in very particular stages. The stages are:

1. Language identification
2. Sound inventory
3. Word borders
4. Phrase borders
5. Extracting meaning

Going through this treatment requires that you to be exposed to the language. It just has to be audible to you. It can be a radio playing, or TV, or any kind of a recording. Just play it the whole day long, as you go about your business through the day. You don't need to actively listen to it: you can have it play in the background. In fact, the more you relax the better. It does not matter what it is, but it is better if it involves emotion, because it is much more likely to get and keep the attention of your brain. The more you are exposed to it, the better.

Do it for a week or a month, until you start feeling like you know the language, except you don't know what all the words mean. It is a very strange sensation, one that I have experienced many times. This is what I used to feel about Chinese: I could even tell where the person's accept was from, but I just couldn't understand anything of what they were saying. At this point, you are ready to go the last stage, stage 5, where your brain will be magically learning what the words mean, or you can even jump directly into traditional learning.

1—Language identification.

How often can you identify what language is being spoken by the foreigners? Many people don't speak a foreign language, but they can unmistakably identify what language is being spoken. You don't have to speak French to identify its special way of rolling r's in the throat,—but that is a very easy to spot sound. How about Danish vs Swedish? Or Azeri vs Turkish? They can sound quite similar to someone who does hasn't been exposed to them.

The first stage of passive language learning, or Learning from Scratch, is to learn to identify your target language when you hear it: to differentiate it from all others. When you hear this foreign language spoken for long enough, your brain starts paying attention. The first thing it will do is recognize the repetition of patterns in this language and register them, just like the human immune system gets vaccinated and can recognize a virus next time it is exposed to it.

During this stage, the brain will very generally study the sound and intonation patterns of the language, and at the end of the stage, it will be able to recognize it among thousands of others. It is exactly like DNA testing, based on several markers. The time it takes to complete this stage varies greatly from person to person, but you can test yourself by listening to other people speak, or look for it online, and see if you can recognize it. If you succeed, you know where you are in the process.

2—Sound inventory.

During the second stage of passive learning, your brain will be working on compiling an inventory of sounds. Every language has a finite number of sound variations. For example, Russian does not have the English sound "w", but English does not have the Russian sound "ы", which sounds like something like a mix of "u" in "put" and "i" in "pit." Sound inventory is not the same as alphabet, but much larger, because it includes all the sound variations that are not reflected in orthography, plus variation from speaker to speaker. Things like aspiration, for example, in the word "hot" and the word "root": there is a flow of air after "t" in the first case, and almost non in the second. Don't worry about the details, your brain will take care of it. It knows what to do. Your brain will register the range of how each sound varies from word to word, and from speaker to speaker.

3—Word borders.

With time, your brain will start detecting where each word starts and ends, and the foreign speech will start sounding much more intelligible. It will stop sounding like a torrent of sounds, but instead like a structure with rules and patterns. It is now that the language is starting to enter your consciousness. You are becoming aware of it. If someone would say a phrase to you, you would be able to tell each word of it—even if you don't know what each of them means.

At this point, your brain will notice a pattern in the sequences of words within sentences. It will also start noticing the patterns within words themselves—what is called morphology.

4—Phrase borders.

This is a very exciting stage, one where you will start feeling like you can almost tell what the speakers are saying, while wondering how it could possibly happen, if you still consciously do not understand a word. This is where the brain is learning syntax, or how sentences are formed, where they start and end, and how they relate to each other. It is grammar that we usually learn consciously, but the brain can do it all on its own, if you just let it.

It is interesting that in Arabic, there are no commas, no dots, and no punctuation marks. If a Westerner looks at written Arabic, they will see a sea of signs, and will have trouble telling where a word starts and begins. Forget about sentences! It is quite impossible without knowing the meaning of what is written.

It is the same with sounds, initially. Eventually, your brain will be able to tell sentence borders. It will register a pattern in sequences within sentences—all the while not knowing what they actually mean.

You will also become able to clearly tell a question from negation, from a positive statement, from a doubt,—all by listening. Many people are able to tell with minimal exposure, just from the intonation. However, there are languages with very little variation in overall intonation: Czech and some tonal Asian languages are examples. There, the raising tone characteristic of questions in the West is not necessarily the rule, or is just hard to tell. During this stage, you will become able to make such differentiation, regardless of your linguistic abilities or the tonal makeup of a language.

5—Extracting meaning.

To complete this stage, you must move on to auditory-visual exposure. While the first four stages can rely solely on hearing a spoken language, now you will need to be able to see people speaking and interacting with each other. The best way is to watch movies in the language you are learning. The more dramatic the movie is the better. Movies create the emotional dynamics to engage the brain, and also offer a simulation of the physical experience that a child has, since our brain can poorly tell the different the real reality and the one on the screen. Both listening to and watching the body language, as well as reading the subtitles is beneficial, in different ways.

During this stage, you will realize that you know the meaning of certain words: you have learned them from the context. Your brain has noticed that they repeat under certain circumstances, and it knows what they mean pragmatically: that is, when to use them and for what purposes. Among many others, I learned the Hindi word "dil" that way, by watching Hindi movies. Every time they say or sing "dil", they put their hand on their heart. I later confirmed it with native speakers.

Things like "Thank you" and "Good bye" are the easiest to learn, and you can learn them with very limited exposure. However, it all depends on the specificity of your brain. If you have a hard time learning such things, then going through a long exposure to the language will ensure that you are able to do it, regardless of your ability and the type of language it is.

At this final stage, you will finally feel like you understand what speakers are saying and feel confident about it. If during previous stages, you were wondering how it was possible, now you have consciously registered your knowledge of the language. Cutting the passive learning period short is fine, it is still better than nothing, but for optimal results—it is better to go through the final stage, before starting with the traditional learning.

One tell-tell sign of coming to an end of this stage is a certain impulse you will feel to enter a conversation and participate. There will be a certain loss of fear in you. You will just know, because of the sudden surge of confidence you will feel.

And now, you are ready to start studying your foreign language the traditional way! After the brain has opened up to the new language, there are specific simple techniques that will make the brain learn it further and retain it. So, what are they?

PRACTICAL TECHNIQUES

Once you are ready to start learning grammar, there are a few helpful techniques you can use, in order to help your brain memorize words and rules, and to get you not only to understand the language, but also to speak it.

There is one condition for any of the techniques to work: do not be afraid of making mistakes! Being afraid will greatly stifle your learning. Do not be afraid of saying things wrong, don't be afraid of someone laughing at you, don't be afraid of losing face. You won't! If anybody laughs at you, it will only be out of endearment. It is hard to do a greater thing to compliment someone's culture than trying to speak their language.

Repeat 5 times.

When you learn a new word, just repeat it aloud exactly 5 times. Number 5 is magical. For some reason, your brain regards a word as relevant if you repeat it at least five times in a row. Anything repetitive is jarring to the brain, and this is no exception: it is instantly considered relevant and important. You have to be careful not to repeat too many times, to avoid irritating the brain and having it block it out like white noise, or as something too invasive and too dangerous.

Dissect words for their spare parts.

Yes, words are just like cars: they have parts. The main part is always the root. Before the root, there is a prefix, after the root—there is a suffix and an ending. Dissecting words into their parts will make you more connected to them, will activate more neural pathways in your brain, and will make you learn the words faster. It does not have to be a heavy linguistic analysis, but rather understanding where the parts begin and end, and possibly, also their meanings.

One simple example of dissecting a word is: "overlooked." Prefix is "over", the root is "look", and the ending is "ed", and there is no suffix. Another example is "premeditated." Prefix is "pre", root is "meditat", or essentially "meditate", and the ending is "ed." If the language written in characters, like Chinese, you can still dissect them into simpler parts, which in Chinese is actually fascinating!

Learn words in clusters of synonyms.

It is easier to memorize words when you learn them in meaningful clusters. Words can be connected in many ways: an activity, a location, or the similarity of meaning. When you learn a word, find its synonyms and read their descriptions. Try to get an emotional reaction to each one and remember how they differ. Some people like to color code, others have mnemonic devices to memorize what the words mean, but for me personally synonym clusters are most powerful, especially when trying to learn a language at a higher level—so that you can eventually read literature in it or speak to someone on sophisticated topics. Then, there are pairs of opposites—the antonyms. These pairs also greatly help memorization.

Make a written list.

Writing lists of words you would like to memorize, crossing out those you have learned also works for many people. The list has to be written by hand, and not typed. There is something about fine motor skills that is connected to word retention. Pay attention to your handwriting: if it is not tidy, try to re-write it in a nice way. For some reason, writing clearly forces your brain to organize itself and memorize what you are writing.

Talk to yourself.

To get you to speak a language, start talking to yourself, as you go through your day, using all the words you know, focusing on the new ones. Try to think out loud and comment on what you are doing. Talk to yourself in a dialogue. Yes, you might look crazy to the outsiders, but it is always a good conversation starter. If you want to avoid that, either do it when no one is around, or just talk to yourself inside your head. As you talk, look up words that you don't know, so you can continue your speech unimpeded. When your brain has a reason to know the word, it is much more likely to consider it relevant and important, and retain it.

Read out loud.

If you can get your hands on any text in that language, and you know how to read it, then read it out loud, paying careful attention to the sound of your voice. You may not like your voice at first, but you will get used to it with time. You can even start acting out the text a little, and that will be even more helpful.

Write in social media.

Participating in any social media in the language you are learning is also a powerful tool. If you are able to write in the foreign language, do write as much as you can, especially in busy areas, with the longest conversations. Just do it and don't worry about what anyone will think about your language skills. Get into it, get emotionally engaged, and it will work wonders.

Listen to emotional songs and sing along.

When you find a melody you like, find the song, find the lyrics and translate them. Then, figure out each word, and try to sing along with the song, feeling the emotion in each word. The emotional connection to the song will make it much easier to learn those words. Conversely, if you have a hard time learning a difficult phrase, just make a song out of it. This is how children are often taught to memorize the alphabet, and is exactly the approach to learn the Quran. Once, I wanted to learn how to say "Nice to meet you" in Tagalog, the national language of the Philippines: "Ikinagagalak kitang makilala". Yes, it was not easy to learn it just like that! So, I made up a song out of it, and instantly memorized the phrase. The song became a hit! Whenever I sing it to someone from the Philippines, they cry. Every single time. Well, at least, they have tears in their eyes, and those are moments to treasure.

Take it up another notch.

When you study, always try to be on the edge of how much you can handle. Just when you feel like you can relax, and it has finally become easy, take it up another notch. That will ensure that you always stay at the peak of your ability and stimulation.

What that means is specific to each situation, and has to do more with your feeling than a universally applicable action.

Eventually, you will start feeling confident about your ability, but that does not mean that learning is done and over. Language is not something you can get done and put it away as a trophy. You can, but it will disappear on you. So, maintaining any kind of exposure is the key. The least you can do is passively being exposed to the sound of the language, to keep it fresh and relevant in your brain.

BASIC STARTER KIT

Getting started in a language is the hardest part. Never mind learning how to say hello and thank you. That does not count as starting. There must be a mental hook that will get you to learn words like a rolling snowball that keeps automatically collecting.

Most of traditional language teaching makes students learn the vocabulary according to areas of life or activities: family, school, clothes, shopping. Traditionally, that is how you start on the day one, literally. Most of the time, you are bombarded with lists of nouns, very few adjectives, and even fewer verbs. I suggest putting that off for later, when you have already learned something more important: a whole blueprint for your new vocabulary. I call it the Christmas Tree model. It has worked for me with every single language, and it makes things very-very easy.

Christmas Tree model.

A Christmas tree cannot exist without a trunk and branches. Ornaments always come second. Ornaments on their own are just a colorful, shapeless, disorganized pile of stuff. And that is exactly how your brain normally feels, when fed a whole bunch of new vocabulary, especially nouns. Nouns name the objects in the physical reality we experience, and memorizing them is like memorizing the names of all the people we have ever met. It just does not scale, since every person is different. Roughly speaking. Yet verbs—they are a whole different animal. They scale, because you can use the same verb in relation to many-many nouns.

You can watch, need, eat, hear and see a lot of things. You can talk about a lot of things. You can tell a whole story. Yet, a thing is just a thing.

Nouns and pronouns are essentially ornaments on a Christmas tree, while the verbs are the trunk and branches. The verbs are essential in starting with a new language, and they are the first thing you should be learning after hello and thank you. Well, it is always good to know how to say I and you, but those often are absent in grammar, because they are understood, and you can also point to yourself and anyone else.

As a new learner, you need a Christmas Tree, so you can decorate it. You needs some essential verbs, which will connect the nouns to each other, and that way you can describe what is happening in the world. Learning primarily nouns will only allow you to point to things in the world and call them names, and nothing else. However, learning a few pronouns with a few verbs first, then slowly adding nouns and adjectives into the mix will make it much easier to ease into a language. That's decorating the

Christmas Tree. You need to start by figuring out the sentence structure in the language you study, and then create some basic formulas for how to describe basic actions.

You can always talk about yourself first: what you do, what you see, where you are going, what you need. You can learn how to say "I"plus the verb in present tense, and then go around saying those things, as you go through your day. "I am hungry" or "I am Vera", for example. Then, you can make it more complex and try to say things like "I need food" and "I am going to school",—it could be anything preposterous or fantastic, too.

It is important to figure out how the trunk and the branches of the Christmas Tree grow together in this language: how the sentences are formed. You start by trying to express your thoughts in that language, describing everything you see, think and feel, and everything that happens around you, as you go about your business the whole day.

In English, a basic sentence usually consists of subject + verb + object: "I have a book", for example.

A question is made by placing the verb in the beginning of a sentence, as in "Are you cold?", instead of simply raising the intonation at the end, as it is done in many other languages. Find out the basic formulas in the language you are learning, and try using them to express yourself. Once you feel confident with one formula, find another one, and so on. Of course, you will make mistakes at first, and will not know endings, conjugations, etc. The hardest and the most important part is starting to build your arsenal of such formulas, as expression tools that you can use to describe increasingly complex ideas.

This kind of formulas work very well. They also work especially when you know what you want to express, making your brain look for an answer, and fill in the blanks of the formula. You can either look it up in a grammar book, or you can ask a native how to say it. It is better to find something you want to say, and then have your brain look for an answer, rather than just feed it something it did not ask for.

Here are some suggestions on what words to learn first, when starting with a language. Learn as you go, and learn as needed and not more. This is like a starter kit that will help you break the initial language barrier, and, once you do, you will have no fear, because everything you learn will have a place to be filed in your personal Christmas Tree, as you learn more and more formulas.

- **Hello and thank you.** These are social lubricants, not more.
- **Basic pronouns: I, you.** Learn the rest of them later.
- **Simple sentence structure:** simple present, simple past, simple future. Example: I go, you want. Those are the formulas.
- **Yes and no.** Those are important for practical reasons.
- **Verbs:** must, can, need, go, like/love, study, speak, eat/drink, need, remember/forget, read/write, work/relax, stand/sit, know, open/close, give/take, leave/return, search/find, understand,

agree/disagree, start/finish, stop, help, begin/ stop, send/receive, accept/reject, get used to, keep/give away, etc.

- **How to use negation.** For example: I don't know, or not this, or not small, or don't go.
- **Numbers 1 through 10.**
- **Colors:** red, green, blue, yellow, white, black, purple, orange, brown, transparent.
- **Nouns:** those you have to figure out as you go through your day, and everyone's story is different.
- **Adverbs:** here/there, everywhere/anywhere/ nowhere, before/after, now/later/then, always/ never, again, one time, many times, often/seldom, inside/outside, up/down, left/right, etc.
- **Adjectives:** good/bad, every, all, this, big/ small, hot/cold, beautiful/ugly, far/close, easy/ difficult, simple/complicated, expensive/cheap, free, etc.

The key is learning as needed, where meaning will help you retain what you learn. Once your brain reaches a certain level of mastery, you will automatically feel a push of confidence, and your brain will start learning at a much faster speed. If anyone is into math, it is the exponential function, slowly increasing, and then shooting up at an insane speed. Starting, and starting right, is the most difficult, transformative, and empowering experience in language learning.

And never forget: if you can speak one language, you can speak them all!

UNIVERSAL LANGUAGE BASE

Strictly for linguistically-minded individuals: this is something to think about, as you approach the active stage of studying any language. Humans do not think in any language, although languages we know may serve as a reference or a guide for our thought.

Thought must be encoded into a linguistic interface, only so that we can communicate with others, but not to enable thinking. I propose that humans think in abstract terms that are all rooted in our experience of physical reality. Humans share a common experience of physical reality, and our commonality by far outweighs our differences. We have evolved to navigate the physical world, in order to eat and procreate. Our brain uses this skill to tackle all abstract thought, including language. I further propose that human grammar is based on a Universal Base of physical experience of objects, actions, and qualities of thereof.

As an extreme Synesthete and Ideasthete, I can see it quite clearly, and it has worked wonders for me, in my own language learning. Synesthesia is a neurological ability to process input into one sense, in parallel with one or more other senses. For example, one can hear music, but also experience visual sensations that accompany it. Ideasthesia is when abstract thoughts assume physical qualities in the mind of the thinker. Both Synesthesia and Ideasthesia have allowed me to see that all grammars of the world have the same underlying Universal Base of physical experience. Each individual grammar is only a representation of that physical experience. So, it is not that the grammar is the same all across cultures, but that their experience of physical reality is the same, which consequently dictates uniformity in grammar.

So, what does this Universal Base consist of? In grammar, physical objects we experience are typically expressed as nouns and pronouns, actions —as verbs, and qualities of both objects and their actions—as adjectives and adverbs. Some languages have adjectives that are verb-like, some put verbs and nouns together, others have particles that suggest a certain quality, without directly stating it. What unifies them all is that underlying trinity: objects, actions, and qualities. Each grammar is just trying to convey the same thing, and the variation is only in the reshuffling of those three.

We can use this model to dissect any grammar of the world, from bottom-up, tracing the ancestry of its rules, endowing them with context and meaning, and obviating the need for blind memorization. It is a much deeper and simpler look at grammar, and one that allows a speaker to go into any language and learn it the way that a child does—

without any help of dictionaries and formal descriptions.

There are some interesting examples of grammatical errors in English that can be explained with the Universal Language Base model. On of them is "him" vs "his." "Him" is often used where "his" is grammatically correct. It applies to all the nouns. For example: "I see him running" should be "I see his running." Who talks or writes like that anymore? Almost no one. What is going on?

What I see happening here is that speakers experience two objects with an action between them: the object who is doing the seeing is active and the one who is being seen is on the receiving side, from the point of view of the one who is seeing. There is a invisible vector that stretches from the "I" to "him". So, if you see "him", then you would say "I see him" + "running" on the side. In conservative English, the vector stretches from "I" to "running", where both are objects, making the sentence to be "I see his running", where "his" is a description and not an object. What we observe grammar do is seeing an action as an object: when "running" is treated as an object, we have to use "his", and when it is treated as a action, we use "him." "Running" could also be seen as a quality, so technically, it could become an adjective in some hypothetical world grammar.

Changing the point of view and any manipulation of how grammar treats objects and their relationships to each does not change the underlying reality that describes the human physical experience. That is why languages are liquid: they change with time, and being correct sometimes loses all meaning. That is why children often create their own rules. That is why children do not care about rules, as long as they get their point across. That is why some languages, like Chinese, have relatively few grammatical rules, and most of the meaning is understood from the context. It is because the context is universal, grammar—is not.

Universal Language Base offers a blueprint that will allow a learner to dissect any language. Then, the speaker can figure out the solutions a particular grammar has devised to describe that same reality. Describing physical events is easier than describing the abstract, although, I suggest that all abstract thinking is done in physical terms, anyway. So, for example, "I hold an apple" has two objects with an action in between, and is easy to visualize and understand. We can very easily tell what object is more active than the other. "I" is more important, because it executes an action toward the "apple", and the "apple" receives the action, regardless of POV. Saying that apple is being held does not change the physical reality of who is doing what.

On the other hand, "I love you" is abstract, also consisting of two objects, with an abstract action in between, but there is a physical equivalent that tells us that they are simply two objects, one of whom is wielding action upon another. "You are beautiful" is really an object and a quality, but in English, it is treated more like an action. English uses the verb "to be" to bind an object with its description, but many languages do not. Russian does not. In Russian, it would literally be written as "you beautiful."

Consider this: "I am happy" and "I am happying", which is hypothetically possible. This is just a reflection that in our perception of physical reality, we often interchange action with a quality, and that can be easily reflected in the grammar. "Happy" is a quality and "happying" is an action—two different grammatical ways of describing the same thing.

Learning to find objects, actions, and descriptions in speech and texts is an enormous step toward foreign language learning. Yet, it should be reserved for the time when one is ready to study grammar.

TRANSLATION

Translation is written, and interpretation—is spoken. Translation, which here can stand for both translation and interpretation, is only a tool to recreate a thought or a feeling in another person. As such, all means are good for it! It does not matter what one says, as long as one gets the message intended. All sounds and expressions are equally good enough—as long as they do the job.

Being fluent in two or more languages does not mean that one can easily translate among them. For many people, that never happens. Some people learn several languages and a fluent in them, keenly attuned to the cultural nuances in each, but are quite unable to translate a concept from one language to another. Others don't have a very deep knowledge of any one single language, but are very quick with translation.

Not everything is easy to translate! Some things simply do not have exact equivalents in other languages. How do you express the Portuguese word "saudade" in English? Extreme passionate longing? How about Russian "Да ну!"? There is literally no literal translation for either of those words in English. In order to be translated, this expression would have to be non-verbally expressed—because there is simply no linguistic English equivalent, except maybe an exclamation "Ah!" or a "No!" And that—would have to be done with a particular falling intonation of disbelief,—otherwise, it would miss the entire meaning.

Of course, there could never be a perfect translation of anything, and translation is necessarily an approximation. It is simply because each word is seated in a distinct worldview, with its own cultural context that each speaker learns over time, both through verbal and non-verbal experiences. To translate something, one would have to feel what a sentence means in one language, and then search for an expression that would produce an optimally similar feeling—in another. Learning to translate equals to creating your own additional language, which it literally is: a system of correspondences between the two you already know. With a little repetition, one would start automatically remembering what those correspondences are, and one's new language for translation is born!

Simultaneous interpretation, when an interpreter listens to one language and speaks in another at the same time, is one of the most amazing things that a human being is capable of! It is worth watching, at least once, before one leaves this world for another. What has worked for me is completely focusing on the language I am listening to, and my mouth does its interpretation job automatically. The second I focus on what I say, the whole process is thwarted. The human brain does so much work subconsciously that we are better off letting it loose, instead of trying to micro-manage everything.

Language mastery only starts with the knowledge of grammar. It is the knowledge of the unwritten traditions: of how words are placed and in which situations, the intonation, and the word choice that will prevent revealing a foreigner in you.

READ THIS!

Contrary to popular belief, becoming a native speaker of a foreign language as an adult is possible. If you are wholeheartedly open to the language, if your brain is willing to accept it as its own, you certainly can. And you will, if you want it bad enough.

www.ingramcontent.com/pod-product-compliance
Lightning Source LLC
LaVergne TN
LVHW052037080426
835513LV00018B/2363